Damn You, Boss. I Quit!

Common Sense Approach to Transitioning From 9-5 to Freelancing/Entrepreneurship Successfully

OLALEKAN AJAYI

ISBN: 979-8-8648963-6-5

DEDICATION

To God Almighty, the source of life and wisdom.

To the mentors, role models, directors and C-suite executives I have worked with, who have shaped me into who/what I am today; Mrs Mabel Toki Mabogunje, Dr. Michael Tejuosho, Pastor Bayo Kolawole, Mr Bode Famose, Mrs Olawunmi Famuyiwa, Mrs. Adelusi, to mention a few.

To the voices that inspired me and guided me along this unscripted path; again former president of the Lagos Chamber of Commerce and Industry (LLCI) Mrs Toki Mabogunje; my e-commerce coach, Jonathan Melody; the disruptive MJ DeMarco; and the first coach who changed my life, coach Steve Harris.

To the inspiration behind the title of this book, the one and only Emeka Nobis, the Don.

And to you dear disruptor and fellow table-shaker, the next-gen entrepreneurs who have invested in this piece. Words cannot convey how grateful I am to meet you and to spark these conversations with you.

APPRECIATION

I want to use this section to appreciate everyone who has played a role in my journey to this point and those who made this project possible.

My appreciation goes to my parents, Mr and Mrs Olajire Ajayi, and my siblings Ajayi Kolawole and Ajayi Olayemi. You mean the world to me.

Special thanks to all of my guardians at one point or another; Mr Bobola Ayileka, Mrs Ayileka Olayinka, Mr Ayileka Oladapo, Pastor and Mrs Beatrice Olatide, Pastor Bayo Kolawole, Pastor and Mrs Yemisi Babasola.

My sincerest appreciation also goes to my editor, Julius Omokhunu. Your contribution to this project is immense, and I'm sincerely grateful.

And to you reading this book and everyone who believes in me and what I do, thank you very much. I am indeed grateful. Let's go change the world, one person at a time.

CONTENTS

INTRODUCTION

The title of this book should tell you already that this book is written by a disruptor and table shaker for fellow disruptors and table shakers.

As such, this book is not for everybody. It is for a few people whose souls have been tormented by the monotonous routine of their daily tasks — aka, a job – which comes with a salary far from enough to live a decently comfortable life.

And to cap it all, such jobs sometimes come with a boss who is frustrating and annoying.

This was my story back in 2019 when I worked as a personal assistant in Lagos. I woke up daily at 5 a.m. because I had to be at the office at 7 a.m. I would get home every day between 10 and 11 p.m. because I had to combine work with the pursuit of a master's degree.

Guess how much my salary was! 50, 500 nairas after deductions (about $150 then — $50 now).

I did that for about eighteen months until I grew tired and frustrated. Then one day I wrote my resignation letter and I said, "Damn You, Boss. I Quit!"

Well, read that as implied — not literal.

This experience, which you will understand better in chapter one, is what MJ DeMarco calls the "fuck it" moment. That moment you get to and you make drastic decisions and damn the consequence, motivated by just one thing: the desire to have a better life and experience.

My desire is to speak to people of like passion; those yearning to redefine their experience and rewrite their story. Not everyone will be entrepreneurs. Some people are equipped to thrive in a corporate and organised setting and that is fine. However, there are others like myself who have a burning desire to be in charge of the systems that create and dispense value in the form of a business. These are people who yearn to explore the world, who are ready to jump on the road or get on a flight when an enticing adventure calls without having to wait for anyone's permission — the romance of a nomadic lifestyle. If that is you, then this book was written with you in mind.

This book contains the learnings and musings of one who called the bluff of 9 to 5 in search of fulfilment. I have yet to arrive at my destination, but I am miles away from where I used to be and partly living my dream life already. You are about to read the mistakes I made when I quit my job, as well as the wisdom I have gleaned from starting my own businesses and making between 7 to 8 figures profit annually.

I desire that the lessons in this book would be like a light that guides the path of anyone seeking to abandon a scripted life for one where you are free and in control of your life.

CHAPTER ONE
The "F*ck It Moment"

Pardon my language. I do not intend to sound lewd or obscene. The words are not exactly mine and I have to use them just as the author intended.

I borrowed the phrase from MJ DeMarco's book **Unscripted**. I was introduced to the path that I walk today by the writings of MJ DeMarco. It was his book The Millionaire Fast Lane that first introduced me to this pattern of thinking.

The phrase is a description of an experience everyone who wants to take this audacious journey must have. And until you have had such an experience, it may be difficult to experience the radical transformation described in this book.

It happened in early 2020 on a beautiful morning. I walked into my uncle's library to see if I could find a book to read. I had resigned from my job in December 2019. So, all I did in that period was to eat, sleep, read and take a few online courses. As I perused the well-stocked bookshelves in the library, I stumbled upon **The Millionaire Fast Lane**.

There was nothing particularly fascinating about the book design but the title got me to stop.

Curious to know what it was about, I began to read. The author spent a good deal of time debunking the old theory that going to school, getting a good job and saving from your monthly income was a sure way to become a millionaire.

His argument per se was that it was a slow lane to wealth and that when the wealth is accumulated over three to four decades, the one who laboured for it may not be in good health to enjoy it.

What a tragedy!

Instead, MJ believes entrepreneurship offers a quicker route to money and fulfilment. He also stresses that not all businesses have the fast lane potential. Some businesses often turn out to be just another time stealer.

The book The Millionaire Fast Lane opened my eyes to the limitless possibilities of the internet and it is the mother of all that I do today.

After that encounter with MJ through his book, I began to follow his digital footprints. I joined his online community and read every book he has released since then.

It was in his book, **Unscripted**, I came across the concept he describes as the **"F*ck It"** event. I read *Unscripted* in 2022 but as I read the book, I discovered that what MJ described as the **"F*ck It"** event was what I experienced in late 2019 and early 2020.

The **"f*ck it moment"** is a period of your life where you are tired of the status quo and you begin to ask questions and seek a better experience. This feeling of dissatisfaction often precedes your moment of self-awareness, when you then gain more clarity on what exactly you want out of life. Then begins your journey to redefining your existence.

Not everyone gets to that point, but there is hardly any disruptor who does not experience this event. When you read stories of people whose parents made them study a particular course, but when they were done, they figured out they wanted something else out of life and went after it, that is the **"f*ck it moment,"** or the stories of inventors who quit school because they were immersed trying to solve a problem faced by humanity are examples of the **"f*ck it moment."**

You might have also read of people who earned good salaries and had job security, but chose to quit that life of comfort to go pursue entrepreneurship or something else – that is the **"f*ck it moment."**

The scenarios painted above show that not everyone who experiences this moment does so because life is tough for them. This experience goes beyond not having money. It is often a case of seeking fulfilment. At such moments, comfort, ego, fear or the feeling of responsibility does not become a factor.

It is that period when you call the bluff of whatever holds you back from living the life that you desire. It could be a job, a career, a relationship, a pattern of thinking, a boss, a system or a health challenge – just anything that holds you back from living your dream. The **"f*ck it moment"** is always the defining period of the life of anyone who wants to walk the unusual path that we will explore in this book. And you bet, it's not always a rosy pathway.

When I resigned from my job in 2019, I had no savings to fall back on. There was also no plan B. But I was certain that the life I was living was unhealthy and one more day, week or month on the job would push me into depression. I knew I had to quit at that point and so I did. But the days that followed were very tough.

On one hand, it felt good to not have to wake up by 5 a.m. to prepare for work and to come back home so late. But on the other hand, I was broke and stranded. There were days I took loans, and borrowed airtime and data just to surf the Internet or do something I had to do. Those are days I do not even wish for an enemy because they were very dark moments of my life.

This is why in the third chapter of this book, I talk about the need for planning if you ever have to take such a radical step like the one I took. It is the common sense approach and a better one at that.

There is a price to pay for unscripted living and the "**f*ck it moment**" is your induction into the hell that comes before the glory.

As you read this, I know you will be wondering whether you have had your own "**f*ck it moment.**" If you have had such an experience as I have described above, you will know it. It is unmistakable. And if you have, congratulations.

However, if you have not, note that you do not force this experience. It just happens. It is like how you do not choose whether to breathe or not, you just do. It is the same with the experience described in this chapter. You will likely have several moments in your life that look like the "**f*ck it moment**" but might not be. They might just be temporary feelings of dissatisfaction or disgruntlement.

Usually, at such times, people complain for a moment, perhaps make certain resolutions they act upon for a while and they are back to the status quo. That's not the "**f*ck it moment.**" The real "**f*ck it moment**" leads you to take radical decisions that align with your dream; the kind of decisions everyone around you will call you crazy for. A real "**f*ck it moment**" is often followed by actions and a full commitment to whatever you consider the pursuit of the opposite of your unpalatable experience.

Again, when you experience that moment, you cannot mistake it; you will know beyond a doubt.

And because, this moment often requires that we quit a lifestyle, relationship, job, or career, in the next two chapters, we will talk about quitting and the right timing for such.

CHAPTER TWO
9 Things I Wish I Could Tell My Younger Self

**As we journey through life, we all make mistakes
and learn valuable lessons along the way.**

Looking back, there may be things that we wish we could go back and tell our younger selves. Whether it's advice on relationships, career choices, or personal growth, these are the things that we wish we knew when we were just starting.

In this chapter, I recount some pieces of wisdom that I would share with my younger self if I could. From the importance of being true to yourself to the power of kindness, these are the lessons that have shaped my life in the last decade and I hope will inspire you as well.

1. Don't worry so much about what others think of you

It's important to be true to yourself and do what makes you happy. It can be easy to get caught up in the opinions of others, especially when you're young and still trying to figure out who you are and what you want in life. But it's important to remember that what matters most is being true to yourself and doing what makes you happy.

This does not mean that you should completely disregard the thoughts and feelings of others, but that you should prioritise your own needs and desires.

2. Be kind to others

Treating others with kindness and respect can go a long way in building meaningful relationships and creating a positive impact on the world.

Keep in mind that the world is such a small place and who knows where/when you'll meet the same people again; if not you, perhaps your children or those close to you.

While I do not completely believe in karma, I do believe that what goes around really does come around sometimes.

3. Don't be afraid to ask for help

Asking for help can be difficult, especially when we're used to trying to handle things on our own. It's natural to want to be self-sufficient and independent, but it's important to remember that no one knows or has it all, and it's okay to ask for help when we need it.

Asking for help can be a sign of strength and maturity, not weakness.

4. Don't compare yourself to others

> "Other people's lives seem better than yours because you're comparing their director's cuts with your behind-the-scenes" - Evan Rauch

Comparing yourself to others can be tempting, especially in today's social media-driven world where we are constantly exposed to the highlights of others' lives.

When we compare ourselves to others, we often focus on what we do not have or have not achieved, rather than celebrating our strengths and accomplishments. The harsh reality is, people's lives are not as great as they seem — especially on social media.

It is important to remember that everyone has a unique journey in life, and comparing ourselves to others will only lead to frustration and disappointment. Instead, focus on your own goals and progress.

5. It's okay to be vulnerable

Showing vulnerability can be scary, but it can also lead to deeper connections with others and a greater sense of authenticity.

It's okay to cry.

It's okay to share a grey experience from your past, so long as you're comfortable with it.

It's okay to be you.

> There are so many success stories in the media already, both the ones that are true and the make-believe. We need more authentic people today than at any other time in the history of mankind.

6. Take care of yourself

The gurus tell you you'd be damned if you sleep 8 hours every day. They scream "burn the candles." Well, I agree, but how far is too far?

Only you can draw the line between being lazy and laid back and when you're pushing yourself too hard. 2019 was that moment for me when I realised I just had to take a break or I'd lose myself.

Make time for self-care and prioritise your physical and mental health. This will set you up for long-term success and happiness.

7. It's okay to make mistakes

No one is perfect, and we all make mistakes from time to time. It is important to remember that just like failure, mistakes are a normal and necessary part of life and can be a great opportunity for learning and growth.

Stop living in the past, for what becomes of you tomorrow is a function of how you deal with the past and what you do with today. Do not spend today wallowing in regret.

Learn from your mistakes, forgive yourself and seek forgiveness where necessary. And by all means, move on.

8. It's never too late to change your path in life

It is common to feel stuck or unhappy with where we are at times, but it is important to remember that we have the power to make changes and pursue our dreams at any stage in life.

It is never too late to reassess our goals and make changes to our paths to find happiness and fulfilment.

Quite frankly, making a change can be intimidating and sometimes scary, especially if it involves taking a risk or stepping out of our comfort zone, but it also brings new opportunities and experiences and could lead to a more fulfilling and rewarding life.

9. Don't be afraid to take risks

Stepping out of your comfort zone can lead to great opportunities and personal growth. So do not let fear hold you back. Fear can be a powerful force, but it is important to face it head-on and not let it stop you from pursuing your dreams and goals.

This book is about taking risks, of course, calculated ones, but risks nonetheless. Every success story you have read or ever will have an element of risks taken by the actor in the story. Yours won't be different.

Wrapping Up

I urge you to reflect on the lessons and experiences that have shaped your own lives as well. While we can't change the past, we can take the lessons we've learned and use them to make the most of the present and the future.

Furthermore, as we look back on the things we would love to tell our younger selves, we can be grateful for the journey that has brought us to where we are today. We can embrace the mistakes and challenges that have shaped us, and use them as fuel for growth and resilience.

And we can be proud of the things we have accomplished and the person we have become.

And speaking of lessons, it's time for one of the most vital lessons in this book. I have said so much about quitting and taking risks, now it's time to answer one very important question people often have on their minds whenever they want to take such a bold step; **when is the right time to quit?**

CHAPTER THREE
When is The Right Time to QUIT?

A LinkedIn connection reached out to me some time ago. He began by expressing admiration for the content I shared about quitting my job in 2019 to pursue my entrepreneurial dreams. He said he found inspiration in my story and was contemplating taking the same leap of faith.

My response was to advise him against rushing into such a decision because there is always a behind-the-scenes to every success story. Usually, every success story has a background story of hard work and sweat— one that is often overshadowed by the highlights and accomplishments.

So, I went on to shed light on the challenges and sacrifices I faced during my journey towards building a successful business and offered some valuable insights that could help him decide if it was the right time to quit.

In this chapter, I'll share a bit of my journey switching from 9-to-5 to being a solo entrepreneur and some of the things I learned that could help you if you have plans to go this path.

In the few years I have lived, I have found that quitting is by far one of the most difficult things to do and there are a few reasons why this is so – the fear of change or starting something new, the fear of the unknown and the fear of failure.

But as potent as all these fears are, I've found out that the major thing that often holds people back from quitting something that is not working or serving them any more is our emotional attachment to things/people — for very just reasons.

For example, how do you tell a person who has been in a relationship with someone for 5 years to quit such a relationship and just move on?

Beyond the fear of change, there is the feeling this person has for the other person and of course, the numerous sacrifices and investments that must have been made. Truth be told, it's a tough one.

Furthermore, when it comes to career or work, some people have spent 10 years on a job that bores them to their inner skin. And you ask, why don't they quit? Because the emotional feeling of their financial security is tied to the job and they cannot imagine what life would feel like if they quit the job that puts food on their table and caters for their needs.

The bottom line is that quitting is such an emotional decision.

Hence, there can be no straightforward answer to the question posed in this chapter.

People find themselves in different situations and at different times of their lives, hence each case needs to be analysed on its merit when deciding when to quit. In other words, a piece of advice that works for person A, may not be beneficial to person B.

In addition, given the same situation, two people may act differently based on their personality and value system. Those are very important reasons why it is difficult to have a straightjacket or one-size-fits-all approach to this subject.

Quitting is an art and like every art, it requires skill and wisdom to pull off.

Because of the intricacy of the subject, I often counsel people to speak with someone who can help them carefully unpack their unique situation. After such a process, usually there is clarity on whether or not to quit; when is the right time to quit, and how to go about it.

Should You Quit Your Job or Not?

Whether or not to quit your job is a personal decision, and it ultimately shapes the reality of your life.

If you decide to take the same path I did, the first step is to make a firm decision in your mind that you are ready to explore new horizons, regardless of the outcome.

Your ability to adapt and persevere will play a crucial role in your journey.

There is a reason why this road is less travelled.

The bottom line is that this decision has to be yours even if someone else's story inspires you. My context and yours are likely not the same, hence you must be aware of your context, your desires, goals, aspirations, and mental readiness to weather the storms that come with it.

But generally, there are often a few pointers that may signal that it is time to quit a job, a career, a relationship, and so on. Such pointers can be gotten from questions like:

1. Does your job, career or relationship require you to compromise on your beliefs or the things/people you hold in high esteem?
2. Does the job or career meet your financial needs or obligations or is it a far cry from being enough? Usually, this may not be a definite indication that you need to quit. It may just be a signal that you need other streams of income, but for some people like myself, this is more than enough reason to quit.
3. Are you making any progress on that job or in that career or are you just walking in circles? If you have been on a job for years for example and there is no promotion, no salary raise, and no professional advancement, then I believe it is an indication you need to quit and do something else.
4. Does the job, career or relationship give you peace or does it mess with your mental health? If a job or relationship is toxic, too demanding and could jeopardise your physical or mental health, there is no wisdom in staying on/in it.

Whatever your answer to these questions might be key to deciding if it is time to begin to plan to quit, or in some extreme cases, to quit immediately.

Planning for Success

Let's say you decided to quit just like I did, I have this advice for you. Before bidding farewell to your current job, it is essential to have a well-thought-out plan in place.

For example, you might be quitting your job to search for a better job/offer. While for another, it may be quitting a job to go start something for yourself. Whichever, the case is. You must have a good plan of action.

The popular saying "he who fails to plan, plans to fail" is relevant here.

I must admit that the timing for when I quit my job was far from right. I did not have any concrete plan. I was driven solely by the belief that there had to be more to life.

For me, I had reached a breaking point in terms of my mental health, and I needed to prioritise self-care and exploration.

While my impromptu resignation had its challenges, it ultimately led me to discover my true passion and purpose. However, this does not happen to everybody.

Also, not everyone walks the path I did and comes out great. Have a plan. Set a deadline on when you hope to quit. It could be 3–6 months, a year, or more, depending on your context.

The goal within this period is to save up some money you can fall back on when you finally quit your job. Furthermore, if your business is one you could do side-by-side with your current 9-to-5 so you can build some momentum before you quit, I advise you to start now that you are still in your job.

For example, in a subsequent chapter, I intend to show you why now is the best time to begin to plan for whatever life you desire and to be intentional about building your brand, aka, laying the blocks for the foundation of your goal to redefine your experience.

What to Expect When You Quit

Choosing to go solo and pursue your dreams often comes with a sense of isolation. Friends and family may struggle to comprehend your drive and the sacrifices you are making. It is important to surround yourself with a support system that understands and encourages your aspirations.

Additionally, it is vital to acknowledge that failure is part of the journey. There may be setbacks and moments of doubt, but each failure brings valuable lessons that propel you closer to success. Focus on the most important thing— keep learning, keep growing and never give up.

Let's take a close look at my own decision to quit and my journey afterwards.

The period after I quit my job had me in between two conflicting realities.

On one hand, there was a lot of uncertainty in the mind. On the other hand, I was making a lot of self-discovery. For several months, I dedicated my time to reading, attending seminars, and exploring various opportunities. It was so refreshing, but, I had to bear the burden of my living expenses, yet I had no stable income. It was a difficult and testing time, but I was determined not to give up.

Similarly, the period between when you quit your 9-to-5 to start a business can be so trying if you fail to prepare adequately. In my case, I quit my job without any savings to fall back on and this made things so difficult for me.

Again — for emphasis sake, if you are nursing a desire to go solo, ensure you have some money kept aside. Begin to save for the 'rainy season' from the moment you conceive the idea. This, my friend, is one of the common sense I have for you in this book.

Back to my story…

Eventually, six months after I resigned from my job, I launched my business, Optimal-Edge Business Concepts. I would spend the next four months pitching my services to prospective clients tirelessly before I got my first breakthrough – a classmate of mine during my master's programme.

Usually, your first customer often comes from people in your network.

I thought that was my break and the beginning of big things. But sadly, things didn't go as planned, so we didn't see the contract through.

In 2020, I attended a coaching program and after the program, I decided I'd stop pitching African clients and try to break into the American market. Good move, but that came with its challenges. The most obvious one is that the market I was playing in before is a different one from the one I was trying to break into; the rules are different and so is the standard, so I had to step up and adapt.

I wrote well over 100 proposals/application letters before I got my first international client. It was a long and arduous journey, but I had prepared myself mentally for the challenges that lay ahead. I had only two options— it had to work or it had to.

But once I got my first international client, I knew I had found a strategy that worked and from then on, I only needed to keep improving it.

The Journey is Rewarding

Despite the hurdles and sacrifices, the rewards of following your dreams can be extraordinary. Firstly, the immense growth that happens to you due to the several experiences you will have is unmatchable.

Then when you finally achieve the breakthrough you have been working tirelessly for, you will look back on your decision with immense gratitude. And perhaps like me, you can look back someday and say, "This is one of the best decisions of my life."

The fulfilment and sense of accomplishment that come from creating a life on your terms are unparalleled. The journey may be challenging, but it is through these challenges that we grow, evolve, and truly live out our purpose.

Wrapping Up

In conclusion, the path to pursuing your dreams will likely be filled with uncertainties, challenges, and moments of self-doubt. You are better equipped if you plan and prepare well for that phase.

My experience taught me the importance of careful planning, mental fortitude, and a strong support system.

Conversely, while the road will not be easy, I can assure you that the rewards of following your dreams and living life on your terms are worth every hurdle.

The freedom to pursue your passions, the fulfilment of creating something meaningful, and the sense of accomplishment that comes from creating your path are invaluable. When you look back on your journey, may you be filled with gratitude for having made one of the most courageous decisions of your life.

So, if you find yourself at the crossroads of quitting your job and going solo, take the time to assess your readiness, develop a solid plan, and nurture your inner motivation.

Be prepared for the challenges that lie ahead, knowing that they are stepping stones toward your ultimate success.

In the end, only you can determine the right time to make that move. Trust your instincts, listen to your heart, and believe in your ability to shape your destiny.

Remember, it is never too late to pursue your dreams, but it is also crucial not to rush into them. Wisdom is profitable to direct.

CHAPTER FOUR
How to Become Anything or Anyone You Desire

Three years ago, I was in a very dark place in my life. This dark phase began in 2017 but became darkest in 2019.

In 2019, I was working in the city of Lagos and studying for a master's degree in media and communications at the same time.

It was such a stressful year. I stretched my capacity to accommodate everything, but I guess I stretched beyond my limits.

Fast forward to December 2019. I was completely exhausted. It was like when your phone's battery hits 2 or 1%.

To make matters worse, my relationship of four years ended abruptly in the same month. Screwed right?

Yes, I was.

How did I respond?

I wrote my resignation letter one morning, approached my boss, who was actually like a father to me, and I painfully tendered my resignation and I was done.

It had been a long year, I was exhausted from my routine, my relationship had gone south, and I had no dime in savings because all my salary went to my master's programme. I was near depression so I quit my job.

There comes that moment in your life when you just have to put everything on hold and put yourself first.

There also comes that time in your life when you know that you have had enough of certain patterns and things just have to change.

Remember how MJ DeMarco puts it "Your fuck it" moment. My fuck it moment came in 2019.

Fast forward to three years later, as I write this book, I have gone from me that was tired, exhausted, heartbroken, bankrupt, and almost depressed to a bubbly, enthusiastic, vibrant me — living life on my terms, doing what I love, making money from it and enjoying a higher standard of living.

Three steps changed my life. These three steps can change yours too.

1. Get clear on what/who you want to be

The first step you need to take whenever you want to embark on a journey is to be clear on your destination.

Without a defined destination, every bus station becomes appealing.

Have you ever called a friend and announced to them you were coming to visit and they asked that you get them something on your way down?

Then you ask what they want and their response is, "Anything".

Too many people do not truly know what they want. Perhaps they have some ideas about what they do not want, but not exactly clear about what they want.

This first conversation is about being clear on what you do not want as well as what you want deep inside of you.

What's the big picture?

Who do you want to be?

What do you want out of life?

What is your ideal kind of life assuming money was not an issue?

You have to find answers to these questions. You need to have a destination in mind.

Usually, it takes some time to arrive at an obvious and vivid picture but you will get there if you dare to still your heart and ask these hard questions.

One of the ways to quickly arrive at an answer is to look around your immediate environment or online. Who is living a kind of life that you admire?

Who is doing the kind of things you wish you were doing?

That may be a pointer to the big picture and it makes every sense if we have one or two faces to it already — the people living your dream life already.

2. Map out their journey

So I'll share with you a concept I learned from one of my mentors, Vusi Thembekwayo. It's called the maps and mirror mechanism.

In this section, I'll focus on the concept of maps as it bears more significance on the subject.

What you need to know in the meantime is that both maps and mirrors are a different class of mentors.

Maps are the leaders and mentors you follow who help you navigate your way to achieving certain results you desire to achieve.

The criteria for choosing the mentors in this category is that they must have achieved the results you desire to achieve.

Who best should guide you to a destination you have never been to before than someone who has been there once or severally?

Hence, for someone to be your map they must have had the results you seek.

To avoid loose ends, someone who has attempted to do what you want to do but failed can also be among your maps because you need them to know the traps to avoid.

But much more, you need people who have results—not theories, results.

Remember our big picture under the first step? The person or people living your dreams. Those are your potential maps.

So what do you do with such people?

The fact is, there is a likelihood that they were once where you are currently.

So your goal is to research their story and find out what it took them to arrive at where they are currently.

Success leaves clues.

This will take you some time investment— even money. But it will all be worth it in the end.

Taking it a step further, if your maps have written books, have a coaching programme or a mastermind, you should make it a goal to invest in such.

That is one good way to get into their minds; and see how they think and experience their lifestyles and habits closely. It is also a way to get into their network and get close to them.

And to the last step.

3. Reverse engineer their success

Having gotten clarity on what your goal is and with some background work done already on your big picture (your maps), it is time to go all out with implementation.

The reverse engineer stage is where you implement all that you have learned from your maps.

This is the stage where you decide which skill to acquire, which course to invest in, and the daily habits to commit to.

For example, if you aspire to be a professional writer like your big picture and you found out that one of the things they did to be where they are was writing an article each day, then it is time to get to work.

You may need to write an article each day or at least five times a week.

The idea of reverse engineering is not to copy exactly what they did/do, but to observe the trends, patterns, and habits they have imbibed and to find ways to adopt/adapt them.

Wrapping Up

One good thing about this step-by-step guide to becoming who/what you want to be is that there is less guesswork involved.

If you follow each step in this process meticulously, you'll have a solid blueprint for execution which reduces your risk of failure.

And while you may not get exactly their results, you will be close. In some cases, you may even exceed their results.

Cheers to turning your life around in record time.

CHAPTER FIVE
How to Quit Being a Debtor and Become a High-Worth Person

At age 27, I found myself drowning in a sea of debt, owing close to seven figures to various vendors and individuals. And I was trapped in a vicious cycle of borrowing to pay off debt. This went on for three to four 'long' years (2017-2021).

Before delving into how I turned things around, the first question is how did I get into so much debt in the first place?

The simple answer is **"bad financial decisions."**

Plagued by debt because of my bad decisions, I refused to let my circumstances define me. Determined to turn my life around, I embarked on a journey of financial literacy and personal development.

Today, I am free from debt, and in this chapter, I want to share with you how I achieved this remarkable transformation in the space of a year— no B.S.

What did I do to change my life?

First Step: I Embraced Financial Literacy

Financial literacy is so underrated in our society.

People hardly hold conversations about how to make or manage money and even when they do, the conversation reeks of ignorance.

Sadly, the two major social systems—family and school—where we spend at least 1/3 of our lives rarely discuss this critical subject.

This lack of education leads to poor financial decisions for many individuals.

Recognising the importance of financial literacy, I delved into learning about money and how to manage my finances effectively.

One of my go-to resource persons for financial intelligence is Dave Ramsey. A second is Tobore Olumoye. You can find Dave on YouTube and Tobore on Facebook. Both are highly recommended.

Acquiring knowledge about money and personal finance was instrumental in my journey toward abundance.

I learned the trends and habits I was exhibiting that always left me in a bad financial situation. I learned about budgeting, investing, and how to make and manage money efficiently.

These learnings changed my mind about money and when it comes to living a life of abundance, it surely begins from your mindset to your money habits.

I Learned How To Make Money

A big part of the getting out-of-debt equation is that you need to make enough money to survive and have some excess to offset your debt gradually.

Sure, you need to cut off excesses and live a very shrewd life but I can tell you for free, it's the slow lane to clearing your debt.

A fast lane is that you need to increase your earnings significantly. As long as your basic expenditure exceeds your income, you'll always be in debt.

During this period I learnt a very basic principle of money: to attract money, you must provide value.

Money is the result of a value exchange. To make money, you must give value in exchange.

This lesson resonated with me deeply. I discovered that to settle my debt and achieve financial freedom, I needed to identify the value I could offer and ensure it was in demand.

Understanding this universal law allowed me to align my efforts with generating income.

So what did I do to make money?

Started a Digital Marketing Business

Yes, starting a business is by far my number one recommendation for you if you want to gain financial freedom.

Starting a business is as simple as identifying a problem that needs a solution and coming up with one. Conversely, you can get a business idea right now just by identifying what value you can offer based on your skill set, professional background, and experience.

Ask yourself, what pressing problem in the world can my skill set, education, experience and background solve?

Once you have figured that out, the next step is to organise a system where you can exchange that service for money.

This is the simplest way to explain entrepreneurship.

I founded my digital marketing business in June 2020. Some 11 months down the lane, I made my first million (1.9 million nairas precisely), cleared all my debt, and from then things turned around absolutely.

Becoming a digital entrepreneur changed my life in unimaginable ways.

The burden of debt no longer weighs me down, and I relish the freedom of being a digital nomad. This transformation is not some Hollywood story or some Harry Houdini magical illusion; it is the true story of a young African who, just six years ago, was buried under a mountain of debt.

By following the strategic steps I have outlined in this chapter, I was able to change my life in record time. You too can.

Wrapping Up

If you find yourself shackled by debt and yearning for financial freedom, take heart.

By embracing financial literacy, learning how to generate income by providing value, and considering entrepreneurship, you too can turn your life around.

My journey serves as a testament to the transformational power of taking strategic steps towards financial abundance.

Remember, this is not a quick fix or a magic solution but a path that requires dedication, resilience, and a commitment to personal growth.

CHAPTER SIX
Three Internal Money Conversations You Need to Have With Yourself

Abundance is a physical reality that begins with a mindset.

Money is a topic that often stirs up various emotions and beliefs within us.

Our internal conversations about money play a significant role in shaping our financial reality.

In this chapter, we will explore three crucial money conversations that can help transform your mindset and foster a healthy relationship with money.

By addressing these points, you can embrace the potential for abundance and align your actions with your aspirations.

1. Making money is moral: Normalising financial success

Society has often perpetuated the notion that making money is inherently selfish or morally wrong.

This narrative is pushed in the movies and discussions that people have daily about the rich; how they make their money and how many believe they owe the society.

Capitalism is demonised. Now and then, this or that journalist believes the rich owe the society as though the rich stole from the society.

These different ideologies from the same mindset lead to one 'implied' conclusion— money is evil.

It is essential to reframe this mindset and recognise that making more money can be a force for good.

Money enables us to provide for ourselves and our loved ones, support charitable causes, and create positive change in the world.

Embrace the idea that by pursuing financial success, you can live a good life and fulfil your deepest desires.

Acknowledge that making more money is a natural consequence of creating value and contributing to society. This will lead me to the next money conversation you need to have with yourself.

2. Not everyone making so much money is doing something shady or illegal

It is easy to fall into the belief that those who accumulate significant wealth must have engaged in unethical or illegal activities.

However, this generalisation is far from accurate.

Many individuals achieve financial prosperity through honest work and by offering substantial value to others.

Shift your perspective and recognise that there are countless legitimate paths to success.

Focus on creating value in your endeavours and understand that you too can make a substantial income without compromising your integrity.

As I mentioned earlier, abundance begins with having the right mentality about money.

3. Recognising your worth: Charging what you deserve

Imposter syndrome and undervaluing oneself are common obstacles that hinder financial progress.

It's crucial to understand that the knowledge, experience, and skills you have acquired throughout your life hold immense value.

Embrace the fact that you are deserving of charging a premium fee for the services you provide.

Shed the belief that you are small or inadequate, and instead, realise that your expertise is unique and valuable.

There are thousands or millions of people out there who would make significant progress in their lives if they knew half of what you know.

You are the missing link between where they are and where they should be

This last conversation is about:

1. Recognising the value of what you have

2. Developing the confidence to position yourself as a premium brand so you can charge a premium and attract premium customers. And you need to do this one without feeling like a fraud because you're not. You're simply using your life lessons, critical experiences and skills to help others while they pay you for not having to go through the long route it took you to get here.

I like how Tolu Michaels puts it, "Don't lower the standards you set for yourself or pretend you're not brilliant just to make other people comfortable. When you put yourself out there like the professional that you are, the right folks will take you seriously and commit to you."

> "It has taken you a lifetime of learning,
> investing and failing to be where you are now."

Your experience is premium and so is your knowledge.

By charging what you deserve, you attract those who genuinely appreciate and benefit from what you offer, fostering a mutually beneficial relationship.

Wrapping Up

Transforming your financial reality begins with transforming your internal money conversations.

Making money is not inherently immoral, but rather a means to lead a good life and provide for yourself and your loved ones.

Dismiss the notion that significant wealth is synonymous with illegal activities and instead focus on creating value and contributing honestly.

Recognise your self-worth and charge what you deserve for the knowledge and experience you possess.

Abundance starts with your mindset and the conversations you have with yourself about money.

Embrace these three essential money conversations, and you will set the stage for financial abundance and fulfilment in your life.

CHAPTER SEVEN
All Employees Are Entrepreneurs

Think about it — no employer pays their employee for your dazzling smile or great physique, with a few exceptions. No, employers pay for the skills and the value an employee brings to their company.

Guess what? That skill set is valuable and not exclusive to your current employer. Other people and organisations need those same skills.

So, think of yourself as a business called You Ltd and currently, your employer is just one customer. If you start a business with all the skills you have, you can serve several people with the same skill and scale your business by leveraging the internet and the connections you have built already.

I know this first-hand because, in 2019, I bid farewell to my corporate job and became a freelancer, building a business around the skills I already possessed.

This has been a game-changer!

If you are feeling stuck in a job that's draining your energy and not fulfilling your needs, it is time to take charge and start building the life you want and truly deserve. So let us dive in and explore how you can leverage your skills and experience to launch your successful entrepreneurial venture — while still employed.

Identifying Transferable Skills

As an employee, you gain a range of valuable skills and experience through your work, including project management, communication, problem-solving, time management, leadership, and more. These skills are transferable to various entrepreneurial ventures and can give you a significant edge when starting your own business.

For example, if you work in a project management role, you may have honed your skills in planning, organisation, and team coordination. These skills can be applied to launching and running your own business, as you will need to manage timelines, delegate tasks, and ensure that all aspects of your business are moving forward in sync.

Similarly, if you work in a customer-facing role such as sales or customer service, you likely have developed excellent communication and interpersonal skills. These skills are critical for networking, building relationships with clients, and creating a strong brand reputation for your business.

Many successful entrepreneurs have leveraged their work experience to launch and grow their businesses.

For instance, Brian Chesky, the co-founder of Airbnb, worked as a designer at a startup before launching his venture. He used his design skills to create a compelling user experience for Airbnb, which helped the company stand out in the competitive travel industry.

Here are some other examples of transferable skills: Writing. Selling. Coding. Designing. Presenting. Organizing.

Making sense of data. These are all high-value transferable skills.

So, whether you work in a white-collar job or a blue-collar one, there are valuable skills and experiences that you can transfer to your entrepreneurial ventures.

The first practical step I took in 2019 was to list all the skills I possessed vis-a-vis the value I delivered to my previous employers using those skills. Mind you, there may still be other problems you can solve with a combination of some of the skills you possess.

List them all. You're gradually drilling down into identifying a stand-out business idea you can start, one that solves a definite problem utilising the skills you already possess.

Now, let's deal with a common enemy that stops most employees from starting a business.

Overcoming the Employee Mindset

Many employees dream of starting their businesses but often struggle to leap due to various challenges and fears. These may include a lack of time or resources, a fear of failure, and a reluctance to take risks.

One of the biggest obstacles to starting a business while employed is finding the time to pursue it. After all, most employees have demanding schedules and responsibilities that take up a significant portion of their day.

However, with effective time management strategies and prioritisation, it is possible to carve out time for your entrepreneurial pursuits. This may mean waking up earlier, working on your business during weekends, or outsourcing tasks that can free up your time.

In 2019, I began taking courses in digital marketing. So I would resume work very early and work till evening before going to evening classes.

While on both activities during the day, I would look for some free time to take my digital marketing program. I also made the most of traffic and the time spent commuting from one place to another.

I hope you're getting some ideas already of how you can work around your schedule in pursuit of your entrepreneurial ambition.

Another common fear that holds employees back from starting a business is the fear of failure. After all, starting a business involves taking risks and stepping outside of your comfort zone. However, re-framing failure as a learning opportunity can help you overcome this fear and push past your limits.

> Rather than seeing failure as a personal
> setback, view it as a chance to learn, grow,
> and improve your business.

Finally, seeking mentorship or support can be invaluable in helping you overcome the challenges of starting a business while employed. This may mean finding a mentor who has experience in your industry, joining a networking group or mastermind, or seeking out a supportive community of fellow entrepreneurs who can provide guidance, advice, and encouragement.

Wrapping Up

If you're ready to start building your own business while still employed, here are some practical steps you can take as soon as you're done with this chapter and book.

- **Identify your skills**: Take inventory of the skills you currently use in your job, and consider how you can apply them to your business venture.

- **Develop a plan**: Create a business plan that outlines your goals, target audience, marketing strategies, and financial projections.

- **Build your brand**: Develop a strong brand identity for your business, including a logo, website, and social media presence. We will talk about this in the last chapter.

- **Network**: Build relationships with other entrepreneurs, potential customers, and industry experts to gain insights, support, and potential business opportunities. You may also want to consider partnering with somebody/people who have skills required for the success of the business—skills that you do not possess, such as marketing, sales, etc. I recently did this for one of my businesses.

- **Manage your time**: Balancing a full-time job and a side business can be challenging, so manage your time effectively by setting clear boundaries, prioritizing tasks, and scheduling dedicated work time for your venture.

• **Seek mentorship**: Find a mentor who can guide you through the process of building your own business and provide valuable advice and support. If you need one, this writer has at least a decade of experience both as an employee and an entrepreneur. Feel free to reach out.

Remember, the skills you already possess and use for your current employers may be all you need to build your own business. If in any case there are other skills you still need, life is all about learning and developing yourself.

So, start learning. And while all of these ideas may seem overwhelming, with the right mindset and the practical steps discussed, you can turn those skills and experiences of yours into a successful personal venture.

I know this first hand because today I have a 7-figure business and it all began with the same ideas I shared with you in this chapter.

CHAPTER EIGHT
Everything You Need to Know About Freelancing and How It Works

If you've ever wondered what the buzz is all about when it comes to freelancing, you are now reading the right chapter of this book.

Heads up, this chapter and the next may seem quite long and mechanical, but it is expected because they are both step-by-step guides and I had to be as detailed as would be helpful.

As a seasoned freelance writer with five years of experience under my belt, I am here to demystify the world of freelancing and give you the inside scoop on how it all works.

Freelancing has taken the modern workforce by storm, providing a pathway to professional independence and flexibility.

Gone are the days of the traditional 9-to-5 hustle, as more and more individuals are transitioning from 9-to-5 to freelancing. It's about the freedom and control that freelancing offers.

So, whether you're looking to escape the confines of a cubicle or simply want to explore new opportunities, understanding the ins and outs of freelancing is essential.

In this chapter, we will dive deep into the gig economy, exploring its definition, characteristics, and how it works. We will cover everything from finding freelance gigs to managing your workload.

Understanding Freelancing

Who is a Freelancer?

A freelancer is a self-employed individual who offers services to clients on a project basis.

Key Characteristics of Freelancing

Independence and Flexibility: Freelancers have the freedom to choose their own schedules and work locations.

Working on a project basis: Freelancers complete specific projects for clients, rather than being employed full-time.

Multiple clients and varied work: Freelancers often work with different clients simultaneously, enjoying diverse projects.

Self-employment and entrepreneurship: Freelancers are their bosses, managing their businesses and seeking new opportunities.

How Does Freelancing Work?

Wondering where to start? There are a few steps to take when starting a freelancing business.

Identifying Your Skills and Services

The first step in your freelancing journey is identifying your skills and services.

1. Determine the specific skills or services you excel in and want to offer as a freelancer.
2. Focus on your strengths and expertise to attract clients seeking specific services.

Creating a Professional Brand and Portfolio

A portfolio is a collection of work samples or projects that showcase your skills, expertise, and accomplishments in a specific field or industry. It serves as a visual representation of your abilities and allows potential clients or employers to assess the quality and suitability of your work.

In the context of freelancing, a portfolio is particularly important as it provides evidence of your capabilities to prospective clients. It typically includes examples of completed projects, such as design samples, writing samples, websites, marketing campaigns, or any other relevant work that demonstrates your proficiency.

As a newbie, a good way to build your portfolio is to create projects for yourself or volunteer to work for others free of charge or for a little pay. Doing this helps you have a few works under your belt — and some experience as well. This then forms part of your portfolio.

Your portfolio can be presented in various formats, including a physical portfolio, on a digital portfolio website, or as a PDF document. It should be regularly updated with new projects to reflect your growth and keep it fresh and relevant.

Finding Freelance Opportunities

Once you have identified a skill and done some work, it is time to begin to connect with your potential clients. Here are a few ways to find freelance opportunities.

1. Online platforms and marketplaces: Online platforms like Upwork, Freelancer, and Fiverr connect freelancers with clients worldwide.

2. Networking and referrals: Building a strong professional network and leveraging referrals can lead to valuable freelance opportunities. Engage in conversations and connect with potential clients and other freelancers in your industry through social media — e.g. LinkedIn, and online communities.

3. Direct client outreach: Proactively contacting potential clients through emails, cold pitching, or attending industry events can help secure freelance projects.

Securing Freelance Projects

As a freelancer looking to get gigs from platforms like Upwork and LinkedIn, there are a few important things beyond your skill and portfolio like the following:

Writing Effective Proposals and Pitches

1. Craft compelling proposals that highlight your expertise, understanding of the client's needs, and your proposed solution.
2. Clearly outline deliverables, timelines, and pricing to give clients a clear picture of what you can offer.
3. Customise each proposal to cater to the specific requirements of the project and showcase your unique value.

Negotiating Contracts and Terms

1. Engage in open and respectful negotiations with clients to reach mutually beneficial agreements.
2. Discuss project scope, timelines, revisions, payment terms, and any other pertinent details.
3. Ensure that both parties have a clear understanding of the expectations and responsibilities outlined in the contract.

Securing Client Agreements and Contracts

1. Once all terms and conditions are agreed upon, formalise the agreement with a written contract.
2. Contracts should include project details, deliverables, timelines, payment terms, and any other relevant provisions.
3. Review contracts carefully and seek legal advice if needed to protect your interests and ensure a fair working relationship.

Remember, effective communication, professionalism, and a clear understanding of project requirements are crucial when securing freelance projects. Building trust and delivering outstanding work can lead to long-term client relationships and a steady stream of projects.

Managing Finances and Taxes as a Freelancer

Tracking income and expenses:

1. Keep a detailed record of your earnings and expenses related to your freelance work.
2. Utilise accounting software or spreadsheets to track and categorise your income and expenses accurately.
3. Regularly review your financial records to ensure you have a clear understanding of your financial health.

Invoicing clients and managing payments:

1. Create professional invoices that clearly state the services provided, payment terms, and due dates.
2. Send invoices promptly after completing the work and follow up on any outstanding payments.
3. Consider using online payment platforms to simplify the payment process and improve cash flow.

Understanding tax obligations and deductions:

1. Research and familiarise yourself with the tax regulations and requirements specific to your country or region.

2. Consult with a tax professional or accountant to ensure compliance with tax laws and to maximise deductions. It is important to note that tax obligations and regulations can vary significantly from country to country. Therefore, it is advisable to seek guidance from local tax authorities or professionals who specialise in freelance tax matters to ensure accurate reporting and compliance.

3. Keep track of deductible expenses such as office supplies, equipment, software subscriptions, and relevant business-related costs.

Pros and Cons of Freelancing

Advantages of freelancing

1. **Flexibility and work-life balance**: Freelancing offers the freedom to set your schedule and work from anywhere, allowing for a better work-life balance. You have the flexibility to prioritise personal commitments and choose projects that align with your lifestyle

2. **Independence and control over projects**: As a freelancer, you have full control over the types of projects you take on, allowing you to work on what you are passionate about. As a result, you can make decisions independently, shaping your career path and professional direction.

3. **Opportunity for higher earnings**: Freelancing provides the potential for higher earnings compared to traditional employment, as you can set your rates and negotiate fees

directly with clients. With skill and experience, you can increase your rates over time and seek high-paying projects.

4. **Skill development and professional growth**:
Freelancing exposes you to various industries, clients, and projects, allowing you to expand your skill set and gain diverse experience. You can continuously learn and develop new skills, enhancing your expertise and marketability.

Challenges of freelancing

1. **Irregular income and financial instability:**
Freelancers often face fluctuations in income, depending on project availability and client payments. It is important to manage finances wisely, plan for lean periods, and maintain a financial safety net.

2. **Client management and project uncertainty**:
Freelancers need to handle multiple clients simultaneously, which requires effective communication, time management, and client relationship building. Projects can vary in duration and scope, leading to uncertainty and the need to continuously secure new projects.

3. **Self-discipline and motivation**: Working as a freelancer requires self-discipline, as you are responsible for managing your time, meeting deadlines, and staying motivated. Without the structure of a traditional workplace, it can be challenging to stay focused and productive.

4. **Lack of employee benefits and security**: Unlike traditional employees, freelancers do not receive employee benefits such as health insurance, retirement plans, or paid time off. Freelancers must proactively plan for their

financial security and consider alternative ways to access benefits.

Understanding both the advantages and challenges of freelancing allows individuals to make informed decisions and navigate the freelance journey successfully. It is important to weigh these factors and determine if freelancing aligns with your goals, preferences, and risk tolerance.

Tips for Success in Freelancing

Here are four tips I have found useful in my journey.

1. Build a solid online presence

● Create a professional website or portfolio to showcase your work and attract potential clients.

● Utilise social media platforms to establish your brand, engage with your target audience, and share valuable content.

● Actively participate in online communities, forums, and industry-specific platforms to network and build your online reputation

2. Develop a niche or specialisation

Identify a specific area of expertise or niche that sets you apart from the competition. By focusing on a niche, you can become a go-to expert in that particular field, attracting clients seeking specialised skills. Once that is done, time to develop and promote your expertise through targeted marketing efforts and showcasing relevant work samples.

3. Invest in continuous learning and upskilling

● Stay updated with industry trends, technologies, and best practices by reading industry publications, taking online courses, or attending workshops.

● Enhance your skill set to offer more value to clients and expand your service offerings.

● Regularly evaluate and upgrade your skills to stay competitive in the ever-evolving freelance market.

4. Manage personal finances

Set aside a portion of your income for taxes, emergencies, and future savings. It is advisable to maintain a separate business bank account to track your freelance income and expenses.

Furthermore, create a budget to manage your finances and ensure stability during periods of fluctuating income.

Lastly, consider working with a financial advisor or accountant to maximize your savings, plan for retirement, and make informed financial decisions.

By implementing these tips, you can increase your chances of success in the freelancing world.

Wrapping Up

In this chapter, we have covered the fundamental aspects of freelancing, from understanding what it is and how it works to exploring its pros and cons. Hopefully, you now have a clearer picture of the freelancing landscape and the steps you can take to thrive in this dynamic field.

Remember, freelancing offers a world of possibilities, allowing you to embrace independence, flexibility, and professional growth.

By building a strong online presence, cultivating a professional network, developing a niche, investing in continuous learning, and managing your finances effectively, you can pave your path to success as a freelancer.

CHAPTER NINE
How to Start a Digital Marketing Business From Your Home

While this chapter speaks about digital marketing, most parts of this guide can be adapted to any kind of business.

It's 2023 and businesses of all sizes are looking to establish their presence online and reach new customers. A digital marketing agency is a great way to help these businesses achieve their goals, and starting one can be a rewarding and profitable venture. But where do you start?

In this chapter, we will take a step-by-step look at the process of starting a digital marketing agency, including identifying your niche, creating a business plan, building a team, and launching your agency.

Whether you are an experienced marketer or just starting, this guide will provide you with the information you need to launch a successful digital marketing agency.

What is a Digital Marketing Agency?

A digital marketing agency is a company that specialises in creating and implementing digital marketing strategies for businesses. They often offer a wide range of services, such as search engine optimization (SEO), pay-per-click (PPC) advertising, social media marketing, email marketing, and content marketing.

That is a simple way of explaining it but it does not get a lot more complicated than that.

Now that we have a shared understanding of what a digital marketing agency is and the various divisions of digital marketing, let's get into the nitty-gritty of how to start a digital marketing agency.

Assessing the Market

This is the step where you will get a sense of what the market looks like for digital marketing services. This usually involves three steps.

1. Researching the demand for digital marketing services

This is where you will look at the current market trends and see what types of digital marketing services are in high demand. For example, if you notice that more and more businesses are looking for help with their social media marketing, that is a good indication that there's a high demand for that type of service.

2. Identifying target markets

Once you have a sense of what services are in demand, you will want to identify specific target markets. For example, if you are focusing on social media marketing, you might want to target small businesses in the local area. Or, if you're focusing on SEO, you might want to target e-commerce businesses.

3. Analysing competition

Finally, you will want to research the competition and see what other digital marketing agencies are offering similar services. This will give you an idea of what you will need to do to stand out and be successful. For example, if you notice that most of the competition is focused on small businesses, you might want to focus on larger businesses instead.

Developing a Business Plan

There is an unending argument about whether or not a business plan is required when starting a business.

My position is that having one or not is yours to decide. However, putting up a business plan is often a good step when starting a business. And while in the end, things may not go line by line as detailed in your plan, having a business plan still gives you some sort of direction.

Furthermore, if you intend to seek any kind of funding to grow the business, you sure would need this business — so why not do it now?

Let us take a quick look at things to consider when writing a business plan.

1. Setting goals and objectives

Before you start, it is important to have a clear understanding of what you want to achieve with your digital marketing agency.

Are you looking to generate a certain amount of revenue? Increase your client base? Create a certain type of impact in the industry?

Clearly define your goals and objectives, and make sure they are specific, measurable, achievable, relevant, and time-bound (SMART).

2. Identifying the services offered

As a digital marketing agency, you will likely offer a variety of services such as social media management, search engine optimisation, email marketing, and content creation — or you might just want to specialise in just one service, e.g. content development. It is essential to identify what services you will offer, and how you will differentiate yourself from your competitors.

3. Developing a financial plan

A financial plan is crucial to the success of your digital marketing agency. It will include things like projected income and expenses, pricing strategies, and budgeting.

4. Creating a marketing plan

A marketing plan will outline how you plan to reach and engage your target audience, generate leads, and convert them into paying customers. This will include things like identifying your ideal customer, developing a value proposition, and creating a content and social media strategy.

Setting up Your Agency

Now you have assessed the market and decided the segment you want to explore, as well as you have come up with a business plan. It is time to set up your agency.

Here are a few things to consider at this stage.

1. Choosing a business structure

The type of business structure you choose will have a big impact on your agency's legal and financial responsibilities.

The most common structures are sole proprietorship, partnership, private limited company (Ltd), limited liability company (LLC), and corporation. Each structure has its benefits and drawbacks, so it is important to research and choose the one that best fits your needs.

It is advisable to speak with a lawyer or business advisor to guide you through the decision-making process.

2. Registering your business

Once you have chosen your business structure, you'll need to register your business with the Corporate Affairs Commission (CAC) or the relevant government body in your jurisdiction. This process can vary depending on your business structure, but it typically involves filing articles of incorporation or a similar document and paying a fee.

3. Decide on operational structure

An important decision to make here is to decide whether you can hire a team of employees or you want to outsource work to freelancers on an as-needed basis.

What you decide is really up to you and factors like, how much capital you have at your disposal. Although, outsourcing can be a cost-effective way to get the skills you need without having to commit to full-time staff.

Similarly, you want to consider building a network of partners and vendors. These can include other agencies, freelancers, and other companies that can help you provide a wider range of services to your clients.

For example, you may partner with a web development agency to provide website design services or work with a PR agency to help with media outreach.

4. Setting up your office

It is time to get your agency off the ground! What you decide to do operational-wise will affect your decision here.

Once your legal and financial responsibilities are taken care of, you need to decide whether you want to rent an office space or you simply want to operate from your house — after all, your business is majorly an online business. Either way, it is time to focus on setting up your office.

This can include finding a location, furnishing and equipping the space, and setting up your computer systems and software.

As you can see, there are a lot of steps involved in setting up a digital marketing agency, but by breaking it down and tackling each one, you will be well on your way to a successful launch!

Launching and Growing Your Digital Marketing Agency

Whew! You have done all the behind-closed-door work of planning and implementing this business idea, and it is now time to launch your agency and let the world know what you are up to.

Here are a few steps to help you keep track.

1. Setting up your digital assets

This is the exciting part where all your hard work finally pays off! You will want to make sure you have all your ducks in a row before you launch, such as getting your website up and running, creating social media accounts, and having a clear plan in place for acquiring clients.

2. Building a client base

This is the key to the success of your agency. There are many ways to do this, from networking and attending industry events to cold-emailing potential clients and offering free consultations. It is important to have a strong value proposition and be able to effectively communicate the unique benefits of working with your agency.

3. Implementing growth strategies

Once you have a solid client base, it is time to focus on growth. This could include expanding your services, diversifying your clientèle, and investing in paid advertising. It is also important to always be on the lookout for new opportunities and stay informed about the changes in your industry.

4. Staying up to date on industry trends

The digital marketing industry is constantly evolving, so it is crucial to stay informed on the latest trends and best practices. This could include attending conferences, reading industry publications, and following leaders in the field on social media. By staying up-to-date, you will be able to adapt and offer cutting-edge services to your clients, which will set you apart from the competition.

Wrapping Up

Are you ready to turn your marketing passion into a thriving business?

Starting a digital marketing agency is a smart move in today's digital age. From identifying your niche, crafting a solid business plan, and assembling a top-notch team, to launching your agency, the journey may seem daunting, but the rewards are plentiful.

The digital marketing industry is constantly evolving, providing a wealth of opportunities for those willing to leap. Don't miss out on the chance to make your mark in the industry, now is the time to start your digital marketing agency.

CHAPTER TEN
THREE Things You Need To Do Before You Start Any Business

Are you seriously considering starting a business?

If you answered yes, one of the most important things to keep in mind is to never invest too much in a business idea that has not been tested.

Without proper research and testing, you risk pouring time, money, and energy into a venture that may not be viable.

In this chapter, we will explore the importance of market research, launching a minimum viable product (MVP) and marketing before investing heavily in a business idea

Market Research is Vital

Market research is an essential step in the process of starting a new business. By conducting market research, you can determine if there is a need for your product or service, and if there is a market for it. The following questions are vital questions your market research must answer before you invest in that business.

1. Is there a market already for this idea? How many people care about this as much as I do?

2. How big is the market available for this idea? (keywords, Google search)

3. What problem is this idea going to solve, and are people aware they have this problem?

4. Does your idea remove a deep pain or fulfil a deep desire?

5. What gap is left unmet in the industry by your competitors? Ask your target customers what their pain points are despite the variety of products available. This is how to come up with your Unique Selling Proposition (USP).

In addition to online research, you can conduct surveys or interviews with potential customers to gather information and insights into their needs and pain points. This information can then be used to refine your product or service and ensure that it is tailored to the needs of your target market.

The Wisdom of Creating a Minimum Viable Product (MVP)

Once you have conducted market research and have a clear understanding of the needs of your target market, it is time to launch a minimum viable product (MVP).

An MVP is a not-expensive version of your product/service that allows you to test your idea and gather feedback from potential customers. This approach is highly recommended if your business is product-based.

By launching an MVP, you can observe and document how potential customers react to your product or service. From their feedback, you will know what the market wants exactly, and you can adjust your plans accordingly.

The goal is to create a product or service that solves a problem and meets the needs of your target market.

A good example is the success story of Dropbox, a file-hosting service. The company began by launching an MVP in the form of a video explaining its concept. The video received positive feedback, and the founders were able to secure funding to develop the product further.

By starting with an MVP, Dropbox was able to test its idea and refine it before investing significant resources in its development.

Marketing Before Launching

Another approach to test the viability of a business idea is to try marketing your product or service before manufacturing or launching fully. This involves putting up adverts or publicity and observing the market reactions to your proposed product/service.

By doing this, you can gather valuable feedback on customer interest and identify potential demand before investing in the development of your product.

Consider the success story of Groupon, a daily deals website. Before launching the site, the founders tested the concept by creating a WordPress blog with a simple offer. The blog received a positive response, and the founders were able to secure funding to develop the product further. By testing the market through a simple offer, Groupon was able to identify customer interest and demand before investing heavily in the development of the website.

Wrapping Up

Before putting time, money, and effort into any business idea, it is important to do proper market research and testing to verify its viability. Ask vital questions about your market, create an MVP, or test your idea with marketing before launching it fully.

Remember, the goal of any business is to provide solutions that meet customers' needs and preferences, and the best way to do that is by listening to them.

So, take the time to test your business idea, adjust it based on market feedback, and only invest in a business idea that has been tested and proven to be viable. With these steps, you can increase your chances of success and make the most of your investment in any business venture.

CHAPTER ELEVEN
Personal Branding Starts Now!

Whether you realise it or not, you have a personal brand. If I looked you up on Google and didn't find anything about you on the first page of results, that's your personal brand. If I found an out-of-date LinkedIn profile or a bunch of random social media posts, that, too, is your personal brand.

People tend to think about a personal brand as bragging, self-promotion, and all about yourself. But it's something much more important.

It is your reputation. In other words, it's how people perceive you — your friends, colleagues, or the general public — and it is what people think about you when they hear your name as well as what people say about you when you're not in the room.

In our connected world, every single one of us has a personal brand, whether we like it or not. This is because whenever we engage with people both in person and online — that includes every interaction or everything we post, upload or comment on — we are creating a reputational narrative about ourselves. Your reputation is already out there.

The question is: Do you want to be the one who is driving and shaping this story? Or do you want the algorithms to be doing it for you?

I think most people would agree that they want to take control.

More so, if you read this book this far, I guess that you are interested in the concept of building a life where you are seen and perceived as being valuable, where you make an impact and you earn enough to live the life you have always dreamed of. If that sounds like you, then personal branding is not an option. It is a must.

Consequently, what this means is you need to make some very intentional decisions and take certain steps to ensure you are building a strong personal brand that serves your intended purpose and propels you towards your goals.

In this chapter, I will walk you through five key steps to building a strong personal brand in a way that feels good.

1. First, you need to figure out what your goal is

Let's start by answering a foundational question: What do you want your personal brand to help you accomplish?

Are you looking to change jobs or transition into a new industry, and do you need your brand to reflect a new skill set?

Maybe you're looking to get a promotion at your current organisation and you need everyone to know all the amazing things that you have accomplished in your career. Or maybe you're launching a new business and you want to build your brand around the products or services that you're offering.

Whatever your goal is, write it down and make it specific so that you are working towards a clear outcome.

2. Next, you will want to get clear on what you want to be known for.

In other words, how do you want people to describe you as a professional? Start by answering the question, "So what do you do?" And I'm not just talking about your job title.

Are you a teacher who focuses on social and emotional learning? Or maybe you are a project manager who is reliable and always gets things done on time. Or maybe you are an artist who makes beautiful ceramic pots from natural materials.

What you want to do is dig deeper into the what, how, and why behind your work so you can make it concrete and easy to remember. Just make sure to lead with something that does not confuse you.

For example, suppose what you do is that you work with families during a time of loss and you introduce yourself online as a "death midwife" People would struggle to understand what you do. But when you start introducing yourself as a "grief counsellor," all of a sudden everyone gets it.

If you are stumped about how to describe what you do, think about how you can stand out from the crowd in your industry. Ask yourself the following questions.

1. What are the things that make you unique?

2. Are there specific talents and expertise that you have acquired in your career?

3. What do you know more about than most people?

Sit down and make a list and you might start to surprise yourself about all the things you know.

3. Now it is time to think about the audience you want to share your personal brand with.

The reality is that your personal brand is not about you. It is about the people you want to educate with the skills, knowledge, and value you can provide.

Who you decide to focus on should be based on two things: the goal of your personal brand and the people who can best benefit from your unique talents and skills.

So spend some time thinking about these two questions: Who can most gain from what you have to share, and how exactly can you see yourself helping them?

4. Here is where it all starts to come together.

Let us pull all your answers into a single mission statement that describes who you are, what you do, who you do it for, and the transformation you can create in people's lives.

Let's take the example of the teacher.

You could say, "My name is Josephine, and I'm a third-grade teacher who specialises in social and emotional learning. I work with students to teach them the skills for fostering empathy and compassion so they can thrive and contribute to a more caring world."

Let's take another example of a project manager. You could say, "My name is Jude, and I'm a project manager for a sustainable fashion company. I work with teams across different departments to plan, organise and direct innovative marketing campaigns that engage customers while also increasing brand loyalty."

Mission statements are going to look wildly different depending on who you are in your career. But whatever your mission statement is, write it down and put it somewhere prominent.

You can use it to make decisions about how you speak about yourself when you first meet someone, in the communities you want to share it with.

5. Let's start building your personal brand online.

There are two key personal branding assets you should think about developing: a personal website and social media (or one of the two — social media is easier).

A personal website is important because it allows you to take full control over your online reputation. It offers the most flexibility in sharing your brand and value with others in a much deeper way than a resume or a LinkedIn profile.

People want to work with others they like, know, and trust and your personal website provides you an opportunity to share more about your personality through photos as well as more about your career and life story. This, in turn, will differentiate you from others in your industry.

Social media is also a great way to share your personal brand with the audience you are looking to connect with. However, I suggest trying not to be on every platform.

Pick one platform that aligns with your goals as well as where your audience spends most of its time. If you are an artist or a creative, Instagram or Pinterest is a great fit. If you work in a more corporate environment, LinkedIn is the place you want to be.

When posting, focus on being helpful to others. Share interesting articles relevant to your industry, post ideas or opinions that can benefit colleagues, and like or comment on posts shared by the people you follow. The key is to always engage in a way that reinforces your brand while also bringing value to others.

Look, I know this may all sound a bit intimidating but try to think of this branding process as an opportunity for personal growth. It is your chance to dig deeper into who you truly are, and who you want to become. This, in turn, will provide you with the clarity you need on how you can make your greatest impact in the world.

Damn You, Boss. I Quit!

Final Words..

We have finally come to the end of this conversation between you and me, but I am very sure I have started a conversation in your head that I hope you follow up to fruition.

Your dreams are valid and so is that desire of yours for financial freedom and the control of your time and life. And now is the time to do it.

The time to start planning your transition is now. And for some other people, the time to quit might just be now. I hope you have enough information already to discern where you are and what your next step should be.

Wherever you are in your journey, I am rooting for you and I believe in your dreams.

Let's connect on social media:

Facebook: Ajayi Olalekan

LinkedIn: Olalekan Ajayi

YouTube: The Optimal Edge

About the Author..

You met me already and read a bit of my story so I'll spare you some of those. Let's get to the part you might not be familiar with yet.

I am a graduate of Mass Communication, at Adekunle Ajasin University. I also hold an MSc in Mass Communication from the prestigious University of Lagos.

I have close to a decade of work and business experience across a few industries, such as;

-Information Technology

-Fashion

-Education Management

-Real estate

-Management Consulting

-Business Development

-Broadcasting

- and Digital Marketing

Coming from a broadcasting background, I transitioned into digital marketing in 2019 and founded my agency in 2020. The rest they say is history, history that I already walked you through a bit in this book.

I am also a Certified Management Consultant and certified Digital Marketer and hold several other professional certificates in fields such as:

-Human Resource Management

-Business Writing

-Negotiation Skills

-Content Marketing

-Social Media Marketing

-Advanced SEO

 I am the founder of:

1. Optimal-Edge Business Concepts, a content development brand.

2. Events & Ovations; a Photography and events outfit.

I am also the founder of a social-entrepreneurship outfit, Emerge Africa, an organization with a vision to empower thousands of African Youths with a global perspective and skills to position them for global relevance.

I love to write, read, speak, listen to music, watch football and travel. I'm open to speaking engagements in any part of the world. I'd be glad to stand before your audience and share my story in a way that is impactful and transformational.

Now, this final part is where the authors say they are married to a beautiful wife and have XYZ kids. Well, I am not married, so let's leave that out for now. Perhaps that would have changed in my next book "S2S." Watch out.

www.ingramcontent.com/pod-product-compliance
Lightning Source LLC
Chambersburg PA
CBHW062353290526
45794CB00005B/2213